SPACE

SCHOLASTIC

SO,
YOU WANT TO BE AN
ASTRONOMER?

Have you eyer looked at the sky on a summer night and wondered about all those bright dots you see? If you have, you're an amateur astronomer!

Astronomy is one of the oldest sciences. It's the study of the universe and everything in it. The main branches of astronomy are astrometry, celestial mechanics, and astrophysics. *Astrophysics* is how the universe relates to the laws of physics. If you have a telescope in your backyard and you look at the sky, make sky charts, or learn about the solar system, then you are an amateur astronomer. If you like to calculate how big a star has to be in order for it to become a black hole, then you're an amateur astrophysicist.

If you want to become a professional astronomer, you'll need to learn a lot about physics, math, and astronomy in high school and college. You'll need to solve problems and apply them to what you're seeing in space.

Astronomer Sondok (581-647)

Sondok, a princess from Korea in the 7th century, was interested in astronomy at a young age. She asked the royal astronomers to teach her everything they knew about the stars. However, her father and other court officials believed that women weren't meant to study the sciences, and forbade her to continue learning astronomy. Sondok ignored her father and ended up correctly predicting a solar eclipse!

Observational Astronomy

- *Observational astronomy* is one of the oldest forms of astronomy.
- It gathers and analyzes data using the principles of physics.
- If you want to look at objects in the sky, you'd use high-powered telescopes, but you can also use radio waves gathered by radio receivers.

Astrometry and celestial mechanics are very old fields of astronomy. They measure the positions of celestial objects.

Amateur astronomers have added to many important astronomical discoveries. This is one of the few sciences where anyone can get involved. What kind of things have you seen in the sky?

Theoretical Astronomy

- Theoretical astronomy comes up with theories about stars, how galaxies form, the structure of the universe, and how smaller particles relate to the universe.
- Theoretical astronomy is a newer field of astronomy.
- In theoretical astronomy, computer models are developed to describe space objects and phenomena that can't be seen with a telescope.

The Light Spectrum

Humans can see light between red and violet on the color spectrum. There are many other colors we can't see that exist in the universe, including colors beyond red, called *infrared*, and those beyond violet, called *ultraviolet*.

Other Types of Astronomy

Solar astronomy – the study of our Sun

Planetary astronomy – the study of planets, moons, dwarf planets, comets, asteroids, and other bodies that orbit our Sun, as well as planets in other solar systems

Stellar astronomy – the study of the stars and how they evolve

Galactic astronomy – the study of galaxies, including our own galaxy, called the Milky Way

Extragalactic astronomy – the study of objects outside of our galaxy

Cosmology – the study of the structure of the universe

Astrobiology – the study of life in the universe

Astrochemistry – the study of chemicals found in space

Cosmochemistry – the study of chemicals found in a solar system

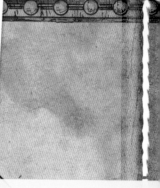

Aristotle's concentric circle theory

A SHORT HISTORY OF SPACE

The Greeks named the stars and plotted their positions.

2300 B.C.

Chinese astronomers record planets and moons.

300 B.C.

Nicolaus Copernicus advances the idea that the Sun is in the center of our solar system.

A.D. 1543

Galileo Galilei is the first person to use a telescope to look at objects in the sky. He observes the craters and mountains on our Moon and the four moons of Jupiter.

A.D. 1609

Johannes Kepler formulates his three laws of planetary motion by observing the planets' movements.

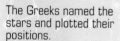

2100 B.C.

The first record of a solar eclipse.

400 B.C.

Aristotle draws a mathematical model of concentric circles for the workings of the universe.

A.D. 100

Ptolemy calculates the past and future positions of the planets, moons, and stars. At this time, astronomy includes astrometry, celestial navigation, observational astronomy, the making of calendars, and even astrology.

A.D. 1606

Hans Lippershey makes the first telescope available for observations. Galileo confirms Copernicus' theory that Earth orbits the Sun.

A.D. 1667

Isaac Newton builds the first reflecting telescope.

A.D. 1680

Newton confirms Kepler's three laws of planetary motion.

Don't confuse astronomy with astrology. *Astrology* is the belief that stuff happens to you because of the positions of celestial objects.

Nicolaus Copernicus (1473-1547)

About 500 years ago, people thought that Earth was the center of the universe and that the Sun, planets, and stars orbited Earth. Polish astronomer Nicolaus Copernicus noticed that the planets did not always travel in the same direction. He realized that Earth was traveling, too. He claimed that Earth and all the other planets orbit the Sun. This is also called the *heliocentric theory.* Many people refused to accept that the Sun was the center of our solar system.

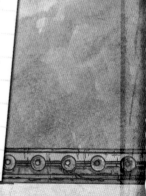

The Three Laws of Planetary Motion

1 The orbits of planets are *ellipses* (or ovals) with the Sun at one *focus* (or point) of the ellipse. This means that the distance between Earth and the Sun is always changing as Earth goes around its orbit.

2 The imaginary line joining the planet to the Sun (called a *radius*) sweeps out equal areas in equal time as the planet travels around the ellipse.

3 The time it takes a planet to orbit the Sun increases with the radius of its orbit.

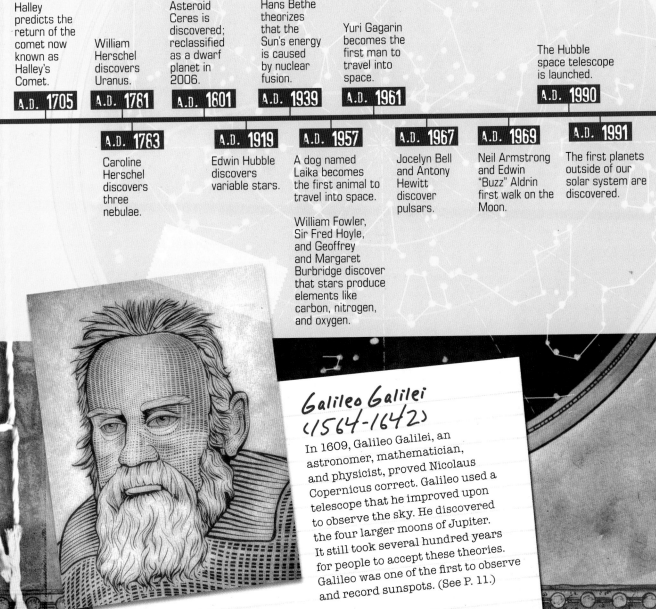

Edmund Halley predicts the return of the comet now known as Halley's Comet.
A.D. 1705

William Herschel discovers Uranus.
A.D. 1761

Caroline Herschel discovers three nebulae.
A.D. 1763

Asteroid Ceres is discovered; reclassified as a dwarf planet in 2006.
A.D. 1601

Edwin Hubble discovers variable stars.
A.D. 1919

Hans Bethe theorizes that the Sun's energy is caused by nuclear fusion.
A.D. 1939

A dog named Laika becomes the first animal to travel into space.

William Fowler, Sir Fred Hoyle, and Geoffrey and Margaret Burbridge discover that stars produce elements like carbon, nitrogen, and oxygen.
A.D. 1957

Yuri Gagarin becomes the first man to travel into space.
A.D. 1961

Jocelyn Bell and Antony Hewitt discover pulsars.
A.D. 1967

Neil Armstrong and Edwin "Buzz" Aldrin first walk on the Moon.
A.D. 1969

The Hubble space telescope is launched.
A.D. 1990

The first planets outside of our solar system are discovered.
A.D. 1991

Galileo Galilei (1564-1642)

In 1609, Galileo Galilei, an astronomer, mathematician, and physicist, proved Nicolaus Copernicus correct. Galileo used a telescope that he improved upon to observe the sky. He discovered the four larger moons of Jupiter. It still took several hundred years for people to accept these theories. Galileo was one of the first to observe and record sunspots. (See P. 11.)

OUR SOLAR SYSTEM

Our solar system is full of planets, dwarf planets, moons, asteroids, meteors, comets, and the Sun.

The Sun

H3 (also called *tritium*, like in Spiderman®)

NUCLEAR FUSION

Proton

Helium Atom

Neutron

Atom

H2 (also called *deuterium*)

Energy

- Our Sun is a yellow dwarf star, approximately 4.6 billion years old.
- Astronomers have discovered that stars this size last for about 10 billion years.
- The Sun primarily is made of two gases: hydrogen and helium. Its light and heat come from a nuclear reaction at its core, called *nuclear fusion*.

Sun Facts:

Core temperature: 27 million° F (1 million° C)
Surface temperature: 10,800° F (5,982° C)
Diameter: 870,000 mi. (400,091 km)
Distance from Earth: 93 million mi. (150 million km)

Nuclear fusion happens when two hydrogen atoms crash into and stick to each other. This makes a new helium atom and a bunch of energy in the form of heat and light.

away, like it does in the core. In the convective zone, energy is transferred very quickly.

The process of solar convection works like a pot of boiling water. Hot gas from the radiative zone rises into the convective zone. As the gas rises, it cools and begins to sink again. Then, it heats up and starts to rise, repeating the process.

Speed of Light = 186,282.397 miles per second (299,792,458 meters per second) (Meter is the accepted unit of measure in terms of the speed of light).

Radiative zone

Radiation in this zone is very important. It's what makes the Sun transfer energy out into space. The energy made in the core is in the form of photons (subatomic or itty bitty particles that travel at the speed of light). In radiation, energy spreads out from the core through these *photons*. They move at the *speed of light*, but they bounce off all kinds

The Sun releases plumes of energy that contain photons, x-rays, and charged protons and electrons. *Flare* activity increases as sunspot activity decreases.

The *chromosphere* is a small region above the photosphere.

Corona

The *corona* extends millions of miles away from the Sun into space, but we can see it only when there's a total solar eclipse. Temperatures in the corona are more than 1 million° K.

Chromosphere

Flare

Coronal hole

A *coronal hole* is a hole in the Sun's atmosphere. Scientists believe that solar winds start in these holes.

Core

The *core* is the center of the Sun.

Prominence

A *prominence* is a large, bright characteristic that extends from, but is anchored to, the Sun's surface, often in a loop. A prominence can last for several months.

Photosphere

The surface of the Sun is called the *photosphere*.

Sunspots

Sunspots are cool regions (3,800° K) on the Sun's surface. They can be as large as 31,070 mi. (50,000 km) in diameter. Sunspots are not well understood.

The Sun's magnetosphere is so strong that it extends well beyond Pluto.

Solar Eclipse

It just so happens that the Moon and the Sun look about the same size when you see them from Earth. And since the Moon orbits Earth at about the same level as Earth orbits the Sun, sometimes the Moon comes directly between Earth and the Sun. This is called a *solar eclipse*. If the Moon covers only part of the Sun, it's called a *partial eclipse*. Eclipses happen once or twice a year, but a total eclipse is harder to see. You may have to travel around the world to see a total eclipse.

Solar Winds

The Sun also gives off a bunch of charged gas (mostly hydrogen), known as *solar winds*. Solar winds whip off the Sun and blow past Earth at 1 million mph (1.6 million kph). On Earth, these winds interfere with satellite signals, power grids, and communication, but Earth's magnetic field creates a bubble protecting us from the worst of the winds. The solar winds will be studied more with the launch of Wind, ACE, and SOHO spacecrafts.

UPDATE: The Hinode spacecraft (pronounced Hin-OH-day) recently discovered the force behind the solar winds. A rapid change in the shape of the Sun's magnetic field starts a wave that moves gas and blows it into space.

Aurora as seen from the space shuttle

How long before our Sun goes supernova?

A *supernova* is a massive star that is nearing the end of its life. Recently, there have been articles on the Internet about our Sun going supernova. Our Sun doesn't have enough mass to explode into a supernova. It's more likely that it will become a red giant and eventually a white dwarf, but this won't happen for another 4.5 billion years.

Auroras

Auroras are known as the Northern and Southern Lights and appear as bright, colorful bands of light in the night sky. Auroras actually are charged, high-energy electrons from the Sun entering Earth's magnetic field and colliding with the oxygen and nitrogen molecules in Earth's atmosphere. As the molecules become energized and then cool rapidly, they emit light.

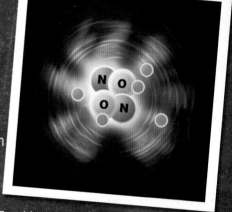

The PLANETS

Sun

Mercury

Venus

Earth

Mars

Jupiter

There are eight classical planets. It's believed that the planets in our solar system formed about 5 billion years ago from a big rotating cloud of gas and dust. In this cloud, there was a fight between gas pressure (which wanted to expand) and gravity (which wanted to bring the gas closer together). Gravity won! The center of the disk clumped together to form the Sun. Further away, smaller clumps formed the planets.

Pluto was demoted to dwarf planet in August 2006.

Saturn

Uranus

Neptune

EXPERIMENT:

The Relative Size of Planets

Let's create a solar system to show the relative size of the planets and the Sun. *Relative size* means how big something is compared to something else.

You'll need:
- 2 peppercorns
- 2 peas
- 2 plums
- A grapefruit
- A large orange
- A basketball

Put the items in this order: basketball (Sun), peppercorn (Mercury), pea (Venus), pea (Earth), peppercorn (Mars), grapefruit (Jupiter), orange (Saturn), plum (Uranus), and plum (Neptune). These sizes aren't exact, but they give you the idea of the planets' relative sizes. Now, take a look at your little solar system. How many peas would fit in the grapefruit? That shows you how many Earths would fit inside Jupiter. How many grapefruits would fit inside the basketball? That shows how many Jupiters would fit inside the Sun.

If you lived on Mercury...

To calculate your weight on Mercury:
Your mass (weight on Earth) x .38 = Your weight on Mercury

To calculate your age on Mercury:
Your age in Earth days/88 = Your age on Mercury

Mercury

- Mercury is the planet closest to the Sun and is covered in *craters* (bowl-shaped dents), just like our Moon.
- Mercury was named after the messenger of the gods in Roman mythology.
- Sometime during the third millennium, the ancient Sumerians discovered this little planet.
- It's difficult to see because it's so small, and the Sun usually hides it from view.

Mercury Facts:

Average distance from the Sun:	36 million mi. (58 million km); .387 AU
Diameter:	3,031 mi. (4,878 km)
Average temperature:	750° F (400° C) during the day; -320° F (-200° C) at night
Length of year:	88 Earth days
Atmosphere:	Oxygen, sodium, hydrogen, and helium
Moons:	None

"AU" stands for astronomical units. This is the standard measurement for space distances. One AU equals the average distance between the center of Earth and the center of the Sun, which is 93 million mi. (approximately 150 million km). It would take 100 years to go 1 AU if you were traveling at 100 mph (160 kph).

Venus

- Venus is the second planet from the Sun.
- It was named after the Roman goddess of love and beauty.
- Venus has been known of since prehistoric times.
- This planet is called Earth's sister.
- Venus probably once had large amounts of water, but it boiled away.
- Venus is one of the most unfriendly places in our solar system. Do you know what it's like to sit on the bottom of a pool? Well, the pressure on Venus is much worse than that. Also, cloud layers that you see through a telescope around Venus are actually clouds of sulfuric acid.
- At Venus' cloud tops, the wind whips around at 217 mph (350 kph), but at the surface there is virtually no breeze. The temperature is hot enough to melt lead.

XOXO
—Venus

Venus Facts:

Average distance from the Sun:	67 million mi. (108 million km); .7233 AU
Diameter:	7,521 mi. (12,104 km)
Average temperature:	872° F (466° C)
Length of year:	225 Earth days
Atmosphere:	Carbon dioxide and nitrogen
Moons:	None

If you lived on Venus...

To calculate your weight on Venus:
Your mass (weight on Earth) x .90 = Your weight on Venus

To calculate your age on Venus:
Your age in Earth days/225 = Your age on Venus

Venus rotates very slowly. One day on Venus equals 243 Earth days!

Earth

- Earth is the third planet from the Sun and the fifth largest in size.
- It's the only planet whose name doesn't come from Roman or Greek mythology.
- It wasn't until Nicolaus Copernicus' discoveries that people understood that Earth was just another planet. They thought it was the center of the universe and flat!
- Earth is made up of several layers: the crust, mantle, outer core, and inner core.
- Unlike the other planets, Earth is made up of several plates that float around on top of the mantle (North American Plate, South American Plate, Antarctic Plate, Eurasian Plate, African Plate, and the Pacific Plate). These are known as *tectonic plates*. The plates move slowly on the planet and give us such things as earthquakes and tsunamis.
- Earth is the only planet known to have water on its surface.

Earth Facts:

Average distance from the Sun:
93 million mi. (150 million km); 1 AU
Diameter:
7,927 mi. (12,756 km)
Average temperature:
59° F (15° C)
Length of year:
365.242 Earth days
Atmosphere:
Oxygen and nitrogen
Moons: One

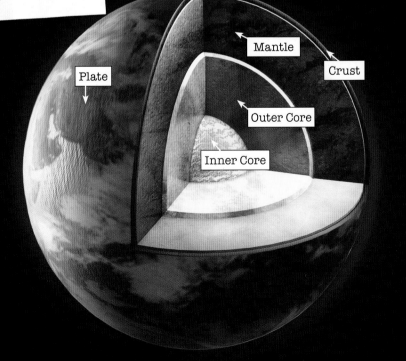

Mantle

Crust

Plate

Outer Core

Inner Core

IF YOU LIVED ON THE MOON...

To calculate your weight on the Moon:
Your Mass (weight on Earth) x .17 =
Your weight on the Moon

The Moon

- The Moon is Earth's only natural satellite.
- Because of the angle of Earth, the Moon, and the Sun, we see different phases of the Moon each month.
- The Moon was first visited by Soviet spacecraft Luna2 in 1959.
- The first landing on the Moon was on July 20, 1969. The first person to set foot on the Moon was Neil Armstrong.
- Earth's and the Moon's gravity pull against each other, creating tides on Earth.
- The Moon has no atmosphere, but recent studies have shown that there might be water ice in some of the deep craters near the Moon's poles. The launch of NASA's Lunar Reconnaissance Orbiter in 2008 will take a look for this water.
- There are two types of terrain on the Moon: heavily cratered and relatively smooth.
- The surface of the Moon is primarily made up of *regolith* (a mixture of fine dust and rocky debris produced by meteor impacts).
- Some scientists believe that the Moon was created when Earth collided with an object about the size of Mars in the beginning stages of our solar system.

NASA stands for "National Aeronautics and Space Administration." This is the U.S. space program.

Moon Facts:

Diameter: 2,160 mi.
(3476 km)

Distance from Earth:
238,866 mi.
(384,400 km)

Mars

- Mars was named for the Roman god of war.
- The planet has been known since prehistoric times, and is sometimes called "the red planet."
- Evidence shows that large floods and small river systems existed on Mars at some point.
- Some recent images of Mars show what could be a frozen sea that was liquid about 5 million years ago.
- Mars can't recycle carbon dioxide back into its atmosphere, so it can't sustain an even temperature.
- With a small telescope, you can see Mars' polar ice caps.

Mars Facts:

Average distance from the Sun:	135 million mi. (217 million km); 1.52 AU
Diameter:	4,194 mi. (6,750 km)
Average temperature:	Ranges from -207° F (-133° C) in winter to 80° F (27° C) during the Martian summer
Length of year:	687 Earth days
Atmosphere:	Very thin; carbon dioxide and nitrogen
Moons:	Two (named Phobos and Deimos)

The highest known mountain in our solar system is Olympus Mons on Mars. It's 16 mi. (26 km) above the surface and measures 375 mi. (600 km) across at the base.

Mars' moon, Phobos, is doomed! Its orbit is a mere 3,728 mi. (6,000 km) above the surface of the red planet. In about 50 million years, it will either crash into the surface of Mars or—more likely—break up into a ring around the planet.

Mars' surface

Jupiter

- Jupiter is the fifth planet from the Sun, but it's one huge planet! It's so big that all the other planets in the solar system could fit inside it.
- The name "Jupiter" comes from the king of the Roman gods.
- This planet was discovered in prehistoric times.
- When we look at Jupiter, we're actually seeing its clouds in the atmosphere.
- The main part of the planet is made up of liquid metallic hydrogen. This is only possible under extreme pressure.
- Jupiter's upper atmosphere is called the *magnetosphere*. It's so big that it extends out past Saturn.
- The colored stripes on the planet are caused by different chemicals and different temperatures. The darker colors are called *zones*, and the lighter ones are called *bands*.
- Jupiter's winds top out at more than 400 mph (644 kph).
- The Great Red Spot is a huge storm, something like a hurricane on Earth. It's so big that three Earths could fit inside it! The storm was discovered by Giovanni Cassini more than 300 years ago.

If you lived on Jupiter...

To calculate your weight on Jupiter:
Your mass (weight on Earth) x 2.36 = Your weight on Jupiter

To calculate your age on Jupiter:
Your age in Earth days/4,329 = Your age on Jupiter

Jupiter's rotation is gradually slowing down due to the drag created by its large moons. Also, this same force is changing the orbits of the moons as they slowly move farther from Jupiter.

Jupiter Facts:

Average distance from the Sun:
484 million mi. (778 million km); 5.203 AU

Diameter:
88,850 mi. (142,984 km)

Average temperature:
-162° F (-108° C)

Length of year:
4,329 Earth days

Atmosphere:
Mostly hydrogen and helium

Moons:
39 (includes four large moons named Ganymede, Io, Europa, and Callisto)

Giovanni Cassini (1625-1712)

Giovanni Cassini studied mathematics and astronomy and became professor of astronomy at age 25. At the invitation of King Louis XIV, he moved to France and became the first director of the Paris Observatory. He used very long telescopes to calculate the dimensions of the solar system. This helped him define the value of the astronomical unit (AU). His value was only 7 percent off!

Saturn

- Saturn is the sixth planet from the Sun and the second largest.
- It was named after the Roman god of agriculture.
- Galileo first observed Saturn through a telescope.
- Saturn is a gas planet, like Jupiter, but it has a liquid metal hydrogen base.
- Saturn is extremely hot at its core. It gives off more energy than it gets from the Sun!
- The rings around Saturn were thought to be unique, until faint rings were found around other planets. The rings look like they are continuous, but they are made up of small pieces of water ice or a rock with ice around it. Each one is in its own orbit.
- Scientists believe that Saturn's larger moons are very important to keeping the rings in place, but it isn't understood how this system works.
- Saturn may have had rings when it was formed.
- The ring system is not stable. It's believed the current set of rings is about 100 million years old.

Saturn Facts:

Average distance from the Sun: 8.86 million mi.
(1.427 billion km); 9.53 AU

Diameter: 74,900 mi. (120,536 km)

Average temperature: -218° F (-139° C)

Length of year: 10,753 Earth days

Atmosphere: Mostly hydrogen and helium

Moons: 34 named satellites

(larger moons: Atlas, Prometheus, and Pandora)

If you lived on Saturn...

To calculate your weight on Saturn:
Your mass (weight on Earth) x .92 =
Your weight on Saturn

To calculate your age on Saturn:
Your age in Earth days/10,753 =
Your age on Saturn

Uranus

- Before you get all giggly, correctly pronounce the name of this planet: YOOR—a-nus.
- Uranus is the seventh planet and the third largest in diameter, but its mass is smaller than that of Neptune.
- Uranus is named after the ancient Greek god of the sky.
- The name "Uranus" was first used by Johann Bode to match the mythological naming of the other planets, but it wasn't until 1850 that the name was used.
- Uranus spins like it's lying on its side, which is different from the other planets.
- Uranus' poles get more energy from the Sun than its equator. But here's the really weird part—it's actually hotter at the equator than the poles!

William Herschel (1738-1822)

In 1781, British astronomer William Herschel discovered Uranus, but he thought it was a comet. William named the planet "the Georgim Sidus" (the Georgian Planet) in honor of King George III of England. He also coined the term "asteroid." It described objects that William found that were neither comets nor planets. He's also known for building the largest telescope of his time.

Uranus Facts:

Average distance from the Sun:
2.87 billion mi. (4.62 billion km); 19.19 AU
Diameter: 31,765 mi. (51,118 km)
Average temperature: -323° F (-197° C)
Length of year: 30,686 Earth days
Atmosphere: Mostly hydrogen, helium, and
methane
Moons: 27

If you lived on Uranus...

To calculate your weight on Uranus: Your mass (weight on Earth) x .89 =
Your weight on Uranus

To calculate your age on Uranus: Your age in Earth days/30,686 =
Your age on Uranus

Neptune

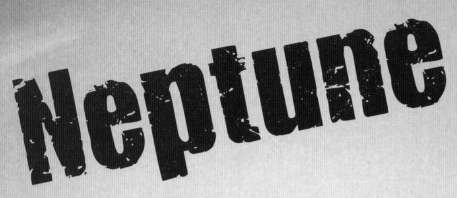

- Neptune is the eighth planet from the Sun and fourth largest in diameter.
- Neptune was the Roman god of the sea.
- After Uranus was discovered, it was noted that its orbit was not the way it should be if you followed Sir Isaac Newton's gravitational laws. So, the search was on for the object that was affecting Uranus' orbit.
- Johann Galle and Heinrich Louis d'Arrest first observed Neptune in 1846.
- In 1989, a Great Dark Spot was found in Neptune's southern hemisphere. It is about the same diameter as Earth. Scientists believe it was a storm. Neptune's winds blew the dark spot west at 700 miles per second (300 kps). But when the planet was observed in 1994, the Great Dark Spot had disappeared. Astronomers aren't sure where it went. A few months later, another dark spot appeared in the northern hemisphere. Scientists now think that Neptune's atmosphere changes rapidly, possibly due to the change in temperatures.
- Neptune has a small white cloud named "The Scooter" that zips around the planet every 16 hours. This is a real mystery!
- Neptune has rings, but what they're made of is unknown.
- Neptune gives off twice as much energy as it gets from the Sun.

Neptune's winds are the fastest in our solar system, reaching speeds of 1,243 mph (2,000 kph)!

If you lived on Neptune...

To calculate your weight on Neptune:
Your mass (weight on Earth) x 1.13 =
Your weight on Neptune

To calculate your age on Neptune:
Your age in Earth days/60,152 =
Your age on Neptune

Neptune Facts:

Average distance from the Sun:	2.79 billion mi. (4.497 billion km); 5.203 AU
Diameter:	30,777 mi. (49,528 km)
Average temperature:	-353° F (-214° C)
Length of year:	60,152 Earth days
Atmosphere:	Mostly hydrogen and helium
Moons:	At least 8

Dwarf Planets

As defined by the International Astronomical Union (IAU), a *dwarf planet* is a celestial body that:
- **(a)** orbits around the Sun,
- **(b)** has sufficient mass and gravity for assuming a *hydrostatic equilibrium* (a fancy way of saying a nearly round shape),
- **(c)** has not cleared the neighborhood around its orbit, and
- **(d)** is not a satellite.

As of now, there are four dwarf planets in our solar system. There are many objects, including Quaoar, Orcus, and Sedna, that may reach dwarf planet status in the future. Stay tuned! Some astronomers believe there are hundreds more dwarf planets in the Kuiper Belt. (See P. 42.)

Pluto

Nix

Charon

Hydra

If you lived on Pluto or Charon...

To calculate your weight on Pluto/Charon:
Your mass (weight on Earth) x .07 =
Your weight on Pluto/Charon

To calculate your age on Pluto/Charon:
Your age in Earth days/90,713.45 =
Your age on Pluto/Charon

Pluto and Charon

- Some astronomers believe that Pluto should not have been classified as a planet. So, in August 2006, the IAU reclassified Pluto and Charon as dwarf planets.
- Pluto and Charon are smaller than seven of the moons in our solar system.
- Pluto was the Roman god of the underworld. Charon was the ferryman who took the souls of the dead down the River Styx.
- Pluto was discovered in 1930 by Clyde Tombaugh at the Lowell Observatory in Arizona.
- Pluto and Charon are double planets, but Charon was once classified as Pluto's moon.
- Pluto and Charon's orbit is really weird. At times, they are closer to the Sun than Neptune. It looks like Pluto's orbit crosses Neptune's, but it really doesn't.
- Pluto is made of nitrogen and methane ice, but Charon is made of water ice.
- Pluto and Charon are a mere 12,000 mi. (19,500 km) apart.
- Pluto and Charon rotate around each other at the same rate that Pluto spins. Therefore, they always have the same face toward each other.

Charon Facts:

Average Distance from the Sun: 3.6 billion mi. (5.9 billion km); 5.203 AU
Diameter: 750 mi. (1,207 km)
Average Temperature: -370° F (-225° C)
Length of Year: 60,152 Earth days
Atmosphere: None
Moons: At least 2 (Nix and Hydra)

Pluto Facts:

Average distance from the Sun: 3.6 billion mi. (5.9 billion km); 39.53 AU
Diameter: 1,485 mi. (2,390 km)
Average temperature: -369° F (-223° C)
Length of year: 90,713.45 Earth days
Atmosphere: Thin and unstable; carbon monoxide, nitrogen, and methane
Moons: Two (Nix and Hydra)

Eris

- Eris is somewhat larger than Pluto and was called "the tenth planet" for a while, with the nickname Xena.
- Eris was named after the Greek goddess of strife.
- Eris is the largest known dwarf planet, and the largest object in the Kuiper Belt.
- It was first spotted in 2003 by a team of astronomers at the Mount Palomar Observatory in California.
- Unlike other planets, Eris has a very tilted orbit, which may be the result of an ancient brush with Neptune.
- Eris is still being studied, so not much is known.

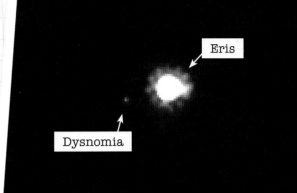

Eris

Dysnomia

ERIS

PLUTO

Eris Facts:
Average distance from the Sun:
6.3 billion mi.
(10.12 billion km); 97 AU
Diameter: 1,500 mi. (2,400 km)
Average temperature:
-418° F (-250° C)
Length of year: 203,305 Earth days
Atmosphere: Methane
(only when it's closest to the Sun)
Moons: At least 1 (Dysnomia, named after the daughter of Eris)

Ceres

- Ceres was discovered by Giuseppe Piazzi in 1801.
- Ceres was named after the Roman goddess of growing plants, the harvest, and motherly love.
- Ceres is the largest object in the Asteroid Belt (between Mars and Jupiter).
- It used to be classified as an asteroid, but since 2006, it has been classified as a dwarf planet.
- Ceres is being studied to determine its atmosphere content and what it's made of.
- Liquid oceans are believed to have been on Ceres.
- In 2007, NASA launched the Dawn Mission space probe to explore Ceres and Vesta (the second most massive object in the Asteroid Belt).
- The orbit of Ceres is slightly tilted.

Ceres Facts:

Average distance from the Sun: 257 million mi. (413.7 million km); 2.77 AU

Diameter: 606 mi. (975 km)

Estimated temperature: -36° F (-38° C)

Length of year: 1,680 Earth days

Atmosphere: Possibly weak; content unknown

Moons: None

Other COOL STUFF in Our SOLAR SYSTEM

Meteors

- A *meteoroid* is a small piece of rock or iron.
- When one of the pieces enters Earth's atmosphere, it heats up and looks like a streak of light in the sky. It's sometimes called a *shooting star*.
- Very small rocks orbiting the Sun are sometimes called meteoroids so scientists can tell them apart from the larger asteroids.
- If a piece of it survives to reach Earth's surface, it's called a *meteorite*.
- Most meteors burn up in Earth's atmosphere, but millions actually reach the surface.
- Meteorites contain a lot of information about our solar system.

Yearly Meteor Showers

Meteor Shower	Date	Caused By
Perseid meteor shower	August 9-13	Comet Swift-Tuttle
Orionid meteor shower	October 17-25	Comet Halley
Leonid meteor shower	November 14-21	Comet Tempel-Tuttle
Geminid meteor shower	December 7-17	Asteroid 3200 Phaethon

Asteroid Belt

- The Asteroid Belt lies between the orbits of Mars and Jupiter.
- *Asteroids* are irregularly shaped objects that orbit stars like our Sun.
- The Asteriod Belt is occupied by a bunch of asteroids and one dwarf planet.
- The asteroids sometimes leave their orbits because of the strong pull of Jupiter's gravity.
- Asteroids can be made of rocks, metals, or a combination of the two.
- They come in different colors, shapes, and sizes, but many look like giant potatoes.
- Four of the largest known objects in the Asteroid Belt are Ceres (P. 35), Vesta, Pallas, and Hygiea. All of these objects have a diameter of more than 249 mi. (400 km).
- Collisions occur all the time in the Asteroid Belt. Sometimes debris from these collisions reach Earth's atmosphere as meteoroids.
- When an asteroid collides with another object, it may create a crater, break into smaller pieces, or scatter the asteroid out of its orbit.
- The surfaces of Earth, the Moon, and other planets are covered with craters.

The word asteroid comes from the Greek and means "starlike."

What would happen if an asteroid hit Earth?

Scientists believe that dangerous asteroids hit Earth about once every 100,000 years. There have been several major asteroids that have hit our planet. About 65 million years ago, an asteroid hit Earth off of Mexico. Scientists believe the effects of this impact may have killed off the dinosaurs. A 100-ft.-(30.5-m-) wide asteroid hit Earth 50 thousand years ago and left a crater in Arizona that is almost 1 mi. (1.6 km) wide.

Even if an asteroid doesn't make it through the atmosphere, it can still cause a lot of damage. In 1908, an asteroid exploded over the Tunguska River in Siberia, Russia. The explosion flattened trees in an 18-mi. (29-km) radius, and was heard 620 mi. (998 km) away. Currently, there are 250 near-Earth asteroids (NEAs), but thankfully, none are on a collision course with Earth.

39

Comet

- The word *comet* comes from the Greek word for "hair." The Greeks thought comets were stars with long, flowing hair.
- There are Chinese records of Halley's Comet going back to about 240 B.C. As of 1995, 878 comets have been charted.
- Sir Isaac Newton discovered that comets move in egg-shaped orbits around the Sun.
- In the early 1700s, scientists developed mathematical formulas to predict the orbit and return of known comets.
- Comets are sometimes called *dirty snowballs*. They are a mixture of ices (both water and frozen gases) and dust that, for unknown reasons, didn't get sucked up into one of the planets when the solar system formed.

- Short-period comets come from the Kuiper Belt. Long-period comets come from the Oort Cloud. (See P. 43.)
- Unfortunately, a comet doesn't live very long in the inner solar system. It melts like a snowman on a hot day! It could impact one of the planets or the Sun, or be kicked out of the solar system by one of these close encounters.
- After 500 or so passes by the Sun, the comet either breaks up into dust and ice or disappears completely.

Caroline Lucretia Herschel

Caroline was born in Hannover, Germany, in 1750. In 1757, she moved to England with her brother, William, another famous astronomer. Caroline began using her brother's reflector telescope to look at the skies. The first object that she discovered was a *galaxy.* In 1787, Caroline was appointed as William's astronomy assistant by King George III. She went on to discover many more galaxies and comets.

Jupiter's gravity broke up Comet Shoemaker-Levy 9. The pieces collided with the giant planet in July 1994. It was the first recorded collision of two solar system bodies. The impact created bubbles of gas and dark scars that covered the planet's sky.

Long-period comets take more than 200 years in their orbit and come from the Oort Cloud (P. 43). A short-period comet orbits within the solar system and spends less than 200 years in its orbit.

Tempel 1

Well-known Comets

Comet	Discovered	Next Visit	Noteworthy
Hale-Bopp	1995, Alan Hale and Thomas Bopp	2,400 years	Was seen for 19 months with the naked eye.
Swift-Tuttle	1862, Lewis Swift and Horace Tuttle	Every 120 years	Produces the Perseid meteor showers in July and August. Its orbit crosses Earth's.
Hyakutake (pronounced hyah-koo-tah-kay)	1996, Yuji Hyakutake	14,000 years	Longest comet tail ever seen.
Halley	Edmund Halley (calculated its orbit)	76 years; next viewing 2061	Produces the Orionid meteor shower.
Shoemaker-Levy 9	1993, Carolyn and Eugene Shoemaker, and David Levy	Destroyed	This comet shattered in Jupiter's gravity in 1994.
Tempel-Tuttle	1865-1866, Ernst Tempel and Horace Parnell Tuttle	2031	Produces Leonid meteor shower.
Tempel 1	1867, Ernst Tempel	5½ years	In July 2005, the Deep Impact spacecraft collided with this comet to study it. Scientists found water ice on the comet's surface.

Artist's drawing of Deep Impact

Kuiper Belt

(pronounced kI-per)

In the 1950s, Dutch-American astronomer Gerard Kuiper made a prediction that there was a distant belt of objects orbiting the Sun beyond the orbit of Neptune. His theory was correct.

The Kuiper Belt is a flat, disk-shaped region past the orbit of Neptune that extends out from 30 to 50 AU from the Sun and contains at least 70,000 small, icy bodies. Scientists think this is where some comets come from. Sometimes the orbit of a Kuiper Belt Object (also called KBO) will pass too close to one of the giant planets and cause the object to sail out of the solar system, impact one of the giant planets, or even go skipping into the inner solar system. The Kuiper Belt is the origin of short-period comets (P. 40).

Artist's rendering of Kuiper Belt object, Quaoar (pronounced KWA-whar)

Oort Cloud

The Oort Cloud, named after Dutch astronomer Jan H. Oort, is a huge cloud surrounding the planetary system extending 19 trillion mi. (30 trillion km) from the Sun. Scientists consider this to be the edge of the Sun's gravitational and physical influence. Other forces, like passing stars, can affect the Oort Cloud, changing the orbits of comets. The Oort Cloud is the source of long-period comets with returns ranging from 200 years to once every million years.

Orbit of Binary
Kuiper Belt Object
1998 WW31

Pluto's orbit

Kuiper Belt and Outer
Solar System Planetary Orbits

The Oort Cloud
(comprising many
billions of comets)

*Oort Cloud cutaway
drawing adapted from
Donald K. Yeoman's
illustration (NASA, JPL)*

Light year = the distance that light travels in a vacuum in one solar year, about 5.88 trillion mi. (9.46 trillion km)

Jan H. Oort

Jan H. Oort made major contributions to the field of astronomy. In 1950, Oort said that comets come from a vast cloud at the outer reaches of our solar system. Oort's main interest was the structure of our galaxy and how it works. In 1927, he proved that galaxies rotate around a center. He then calculated the distance of the Sun from the center of our galaxy at 30,000 light years.

OUR GALAXY:
THE MILKY WAY

The Milky Way galaxy is a large, disk-shaped grouping of stars. It's a *spiral galaxy* (See P. 54), with several arms coiling around a central bulge. Stars in the central bulge are close together. Our solar system sits on one of the spiral arms, which also contain clouds of interstellar gas and dust. The entire galaxy is about 100,000 light years in diameter. It's estimated that

Is there life out there?
During the 1990s, astronomers used new techniques to detect large planets orbiting nearby stars. The search for life in outer space goes on.

the Milky Way galaxy is about 13.6 billion years old. The Milky Way contains about 400 billion stars. You can even see the Milky Way on a clear, moonless summer night. It appears as an illuminated band circling the northeastern and southeastern horizon. The center of our galaxy is about 25,000 light years from our Sun.

Star Life Cycle

Nebula
Stars are born in *nebulae*.

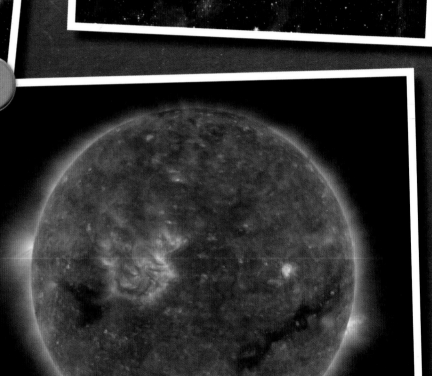

Young Stars
These huge clouds of dust and gas collapse under gravitational forces to form *protostars*.

Main Sequence Stars
Stars like our Sun have no problem changing hydrogen atoms to helium atoms in their core. The more massive a star is, the brighter and bluer it is. Sirius, the dog star, is more massive than the Sun, so it appears bluer. Proxima Centauri is less massive, so it looks redder and less bright.

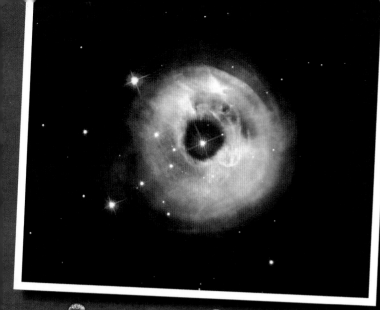

Red Giant or Super Red Giant

As the core runs out of hydrogen and helium, the core contracts and the outer layers expand and become less bright. When our Sun becomes a *Red Giant*, it will gobble up Earth.

End of the life for a Sunlike star

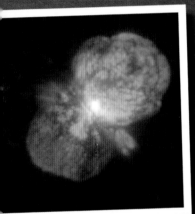

Supernova

If a star is massive, it will become a *Super Red Giant*. It will burn helium to carbon, and then when the helium is used up, it will burn carbon to oxygen and other elements. The dense core releases *neutrinos* and will eventually collapse and explode. The deaths of these massive stars produce carbon, oxygen, and other elements that make life possible.

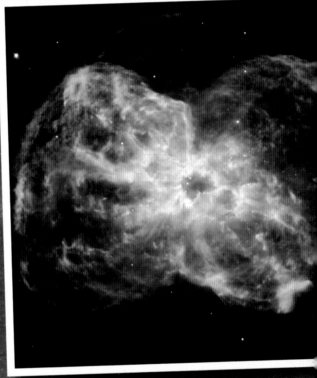

Different Types of Stars

When astronomers look through their telescopes, how do they make sense of all those bright dots out there? Well, just like biologists classify plants and animals by grouping them into specific categories, stars are classified, too. Stars are grouped according to their spectra. A *spectrum* (plural for spectra) is how bright the object is at different wavelengths. (See P. 5.) A star's spectrum shows how bright it appears from Earth. The *wavelength* is the color from ultraviolet to infrared. This information tells the astronomer how far away the star is and what kind of star it might be.

Neutron Star

When a massive star collapses, the atoms are crushed and the electrons are jammed inside the protons to form a star made up entirely of neutrons. This tiny star ends up being a giant nucleus with no empty space. The magnetic field around a neutron star is very strong.

Pulsars

Pulsars are neutron stars that are rotating very fast and pulsing radio waves. Pulsars were first seen by radio astronomers in 1967. There are approximately 1,000 known pulsars. There is a pulsar in the Crab Nebula.

Black Holes

Black holes are one of the coolest phenomena in space. There are several different types of black holes. Stellar black holes form at the end of the life of a massive star. Mid-mass black holes are created at the end of the life of a *supermassive* star and only recently have been discovered. It's believed that there are black holes in the centers of galaxies, too.

Supermassive = made up from a mass of about a billion Suns.

Stellar Black Holes

When a star that has a mass of at least three of our Suns collapses, the core forms a deep gravitational warp, or *black hole*. The boundary at the edge of a black hole is called the *event horizon*. Anything that passes beyond this point will be crushed by the gravitational force, like squeezing a soda can in your hand. No visible light escapes. Looking for black holes is really difficult, so it's a huge deal when one is located.

Supermassive Black Holes

Supermassive black holes are located at the center of galaxies. They are huge, with extremely powerful gravitational fields. Astronomers have found evidence of these black holes by watching how fast the stars or gas clouds orbit these centers. The faster the stars move, the more evidence of a strong gravitational field and a huge amount of energy. The stars move in a way that's similar to the movement of water when a toilet is flushed. It's unknown how these black holes get started, but it is thought that an individual starlike black hole forms and swallows up all the matter

A gravitational field is the space around an object that has mass, within which another object that has mass experiences the force of attraction.

Quasars

Quasar is short for "quasistellar radio sources" (meaning "starlike radio sources"). In the 1960s, objects were found that emitted radio waves with really weird spectra. They found this was due to the fact that they were so far away. Quasars give off more energy than 100 normal galaxies. These objects have extremely bright centers, where some sort of energetic action is happening. Scientists believe that supermassive black holes can result in very active areas where a huge amount of energy is released, powering the quasar. It's believed that galaxies may act as quasars only during the early stages of their lives.

Red Dwarfs

- *Red dwarf stars* are main sequence stars like our Sun, but they have much less mass.
- Astronomers believe that most stars in the Milky Way are red dwarf stars and are 50 times fainter than our Sun.
- Red dwarf stars were discovered only recently because of the improvement in technology.
- Red dwarfs are totally *convective stars*. This means that the energy created by fusion is carried to the surface in a circular motion, just like our Sun, but not as strong. (See P. 10.)

White Dwarfs

Eventually, a star will lose all mass and leave behind a hot core of carbon stuck in a cloud of expelled gas, called a *planetary nebula*. As the core cools, it will become a white dwarf.

Other dwarf stars...

Black Dwarf

Black dwarf stars are a theory. Some astronomers believe that when a white dwarf cools and no longer emits any heat or light, it will become a black dwarf. However, the time it takes for a white dwarf to cool is longer than the universe has been in existence!

Brown Dwarf

Brown dwarfs are formed when gas contracts to form a star, but does not possess enough mass to start and maintain nuclear fusion. It's like trying to start a Corvette with a go-kart motor.

Star Cluster

Star clusters are groups of stars bound together by gravity. Two distinct types of star clusters can be seen: globular clusters and open clusters. *Globular clusters* are tight groups of hundreds of thousands of very old stars, while *open clusters* generally contain less than a few hundred members and often are very young.

Binary Star System

A *binary star system* consists of two stars that orbit around a common point, called the *center of mass*. Five to 10 percent of the stars visible to us are binary stars.

Variable Star

Variable stars change the amount of light they give off. There are about 30,000 known variable stars, which are grouped into three classes: pulsating variables, eruptive variables (caused by a physical change within the star), and eclipsing variables (caused by two or more bodies eclipsing one another).

THE UNIVERSE

The universe is made up of hundreds of billions of different galaxies. When other galaxies were discovered, they were called *island universes* because they looked like islands of stars in a dark sea. Galaxies have a huge size range. They can be extremely large or extremely small. The smaller galaxies are difficult to find. But with the help of the Hubble space telescope, which allows us to see deep into space, new galaxies are discovered all the time.

Dark Matter

Dark matter is one of the hottest topics in astrophysics today. Basically, the mass of the universe doesn't give off or absorb light. No one really knows what it's made of. Scientists believe that the bulk of the universe is made up of dark matter, but it can't be seen or detected with our current technology.

Matter vs. Antimatter

Sounds like a superhero and supervillain, doesn't it? Actually, antimatter is the opposite of normal matter (things that you can touch and feel). It's believed that if matter and antimatter come in contact with each other, they will annihilate each other or produce another particle with a lot of energy or maybe even high-energy photons.

Other GALAXIES...

"Space is big. Really big. You just won't believe how vastly, hugely, mindboggingly big it is. I mean, you may think it's a long way down the road to the chemist, but that's just peanuts to space."
— *Douglas Adams*

Different Kinds of Galaxies

Spiral Galaxy
- Our galaxy has arms that spiral out from the center. These arms contain younger stars and gas.
- All the stars in the arms orbit the center of the galaxy. The Sun takes about 200 million years to complete one orbit.
- About 30 percent of all galaxies are a form of a spiral galaxy.
- Some have arms that spiral from the center, but others have what are called *bars*. The arms originate from the ends.
- Spiral galaxies are rich in gas and dust.

Elliptical Galaxy
- The majority of galaxies are flattened, oval disks.
- They have only a few young stars, dust, and gas.
- Elliptical galaxies come in a wide range of sizes, from extremely massive to small, globular clusters.

Irregular Galaxy

- Irregular galaxies are neither ellipses nor spirals. They have very little symmetry (the same on both sides).

- It's thought that these galaxies have been influenced by other nearby galaxies.

Active Galaxies

- Some galaxies have huge amounts of energy near their center, or *nucleus*.
- These active centers give out strong *radio signals*.
- If a galaxy is extremely active at its center, it's called a quasar. (See P. 48.)
- The centers of these active galaxies are the brightest known objects in the universe. They are so bright that they can be seen from extremely far away.
- The light that we see coming from the most distant active galaxies started when the universe was very young.

Galaxy Clusters

- There are many galaxy clusters. New ones are discovered every day.
- Some galaxy clusters can be seen with an amateur telescope.
- Clusters of galaxies can be seen all the way out to the distant reaches of our universe.
- Some clusters contain thousands of galaxies.

- It's thought that galaxy clusters form when several galaxies collide and combine.
- Studies show that there is very hot gas between galaxy clusters.
- One of the greatest mysteries with galaxy clusters is how they are held together.

Galactic pile-up

Crash, bang, boom! When two or more galaxies run into each other, a *galactic pile-up* occurs. Five billion light years from Earth, four galaxies crashed into each other, resulting in a monster galaxy with stars spilling out into space.

Galactic cannibalism

Galaxies don't always crash into each other. Sometimes one galaxy has a stronger gravitational force than the other, and the larger galaxy pulls the little one into it.

In a few billion years,

our galaxy will be part of a galactic pile-up. Scientists have calculated that our Milky Way galaxy and the Andromeda galaxy will eventually collide to form a single, giant elliptical galaxy. The two galaxies are approaching each other at 75 miles per second (120 kps). Their spiral arms will merge in about two million years. The black holes at the center of each galaxy will combine as a supermassive black hole, possibly resulting in a powerful quasar. Computer models suggest that our solar system will survive the merger, but will be thrown into the distant outer halo of the new combined galaxy. No one really knows what this might do to our little planet!

A LOOK INTO SPACE

BARNARD 30

Barnard 30 is located in the head of the constellation Orion. This is the result of a supernova explosion more than three million years ago. The Barnard cluster is more than 1,300 light years from Earth.

On the outer edge of our galaxy, 20,000 light years away from Earth is a highly unusual variable star. In 2002, the star suddenly began to get larger and brighter, becoming a Super Red Giant. The light from the outbursts bounced off the surrounding dust, creating a *light echo*. (See Super Red Giant, P. 47.)

THE "ROTTEN EGG" NEBULA

The Rotten Egg Nebula is in the constellation Puppis. The Sunlike star is near the end of its life. The star is transforming from a Red Giant star to a planetary nebula. Gas and dust are blowing out in two different directions. The gas is traveling at 450,000 mph (724,050 kph). It is called The Rotten Egg Nebula because the gas is filled with a huge amount of sulfur, which smells like rotten eggs.

M51 WHIRLPOOL GALAXY
and Companion

The Whirlpool galaxy is one of the most well-known spiral galaxies. It was discovered in 1733 by Charles Messier. M51 is approximately 37 million light years away. The smaller companion galaxy, NGC5195, is interacting with the Whirlpool galaxy, creating young stars. This classic spiral galaxy has a dust disk in the center that might feed a black hole.

YOUNG GALAXIES

These galaxies formed when the universe was 12 billion years old. This is a great sample of galaxies in the early universe. These galaxies are considerably smaller than today's giant galaxies. It has taken the light from these early galaxies 13 billion years to reach Earth.

The Orion Nebula is a huge, interstellar molecular cloud that lies 1,500 light years away from Earth. This stellar nursery has a hot, central star cluster, called the Trapezium. The nebula's gas slowly flows away from the star cluster.